WORLD RELIGIONS
MADE EASY

Paul Carden, General Editor

World Religions Made Easy
©2018 Rose Publishing, LLC

Rose Publishing, LLC
P.O. Box 3473
Peabody, Massachusetts 01961-3473 USA
www.hendricksonrose.com

General Editor: Paul Carden.

The publishers gratefully acknowledge the editorial contributions of the following authors and researchers: Mark Albrecht, Brooks Alexander, James Bjornstad, Robert M. Bowman Jr., Christy Darlington, Bruce Green, Timothy Paul Jones, John Kennah, Tim Martin, Bill McKeever, Marcia Montenegro, Eric Pement, H. L. Richard, James Stephens, András Szalai, and J. Isamu Yamamoto.

Cover and layout design by Cristalle Kishi.

Photos provided by Shutterstock.com; Book of Shadows photo by Midnightblueowl at English Wikipedia.

Printed in the United States of America
010718VP

CONTENTS

KEY PERSON/FOUNDER, DATE, LOCATION

Jesus Christ. Founded about AD 30–33, in Judea (present-day Israel), under the Roman Empire. Followers of Jesus Christ became known as Christians.

WHO IS GOD?

The one God is Triune (one God in three persons, not three gods): Father, Son, and Holy Spirit. God is a spiritual being without a physical body. He is personal and involved with people. He created the universe out of nothing. He is eternal, changeless, holy, loving, and perfect. The title "God" is often used to designate God the Father, the first person of the Trinity.

WHO IS JESUS?

Jesus is God, the second person of the Trinity. As God the Son, he was never created and has always existed. He is fully God and fully man (the two natures joined, not mixed). As the second

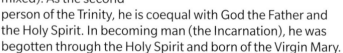

person of the Trinity, he is coequal with God the Father and the Holy Spirit. In becoming man (the Incarnation), he was begotten through the Holy Spirit and born of the Virgin Mary.

Jesus is the only way to the Father, salvation, and eternal life. He died on a cross according to God's plan, as the full sacrifice and payment for our sins. He rose from the dead on the third day, spiritually and physically immortal. For the next 40 days he was seen by more than 500 eyewitnesses. His wounds were tangible, and he ate meals. He physically ascended to heaven. Jesus will come again visibly and physically at the end of time to establish God's kingdom and judge the world.

WHO IS THE HOLY SPIRIT?
The Holy Spirit is God, the third person of the Trinity. The Holy Spirit is a person, not a force or energy field. He comforts, grieves, reproves, convicts, guides, teaches, and fills Christians. He is not the Father, nor is he the Son (Jesus Christ).

HOW TO BE SAVED
Salvation is by God's grace, not earned by an individual's good works. Salvation must be received by faith—that is, people must trust sincerely that Jesus died to pay for their sins and then physically rose again, which assures believers of forgiveness and resurrection of the body. This is God's loving plan to forgive sinful people.

Key Writings

The Holy Bible, divided into

- the Old Testament: 39 books written mainly in Hebrew and Aramaic
- the New Testament: 27 books written in Greek

Major Celebrations

- Easter, commemorating Jesus' resurrection (annual; dates vary)

- Christmas, commemorating Jesus' birth (annual; December 25)

WHAT HAPPENS AFTER DEATH?

Believers go to be with Jesus, where they await the final judgment. Both saved and lost people will be resurrected. Those who are saved will live forever with Jesus in heaven. Those who are lost will suffer the torment of eternal separation from God (hell). Jesus' bodily resurrection guarantees believers that they, too, will be resurrected and receive new, immortal bodies.

OTHER FACTS, BELIEFS, OR PRACTICES

Group worship, usually held in churches. No secret rites or doctrines. Baptism and the Lord's Supper (Communion). Active voluntary missionary efforts. Aid to those in need: the poor, widows, orphans, and downtrodden.

Christians believe that Jesus is the Jewish Messiah promised to Israel in the Old Testament (*Tanakh*). Jesus said that his followers would be known by their love for one another. Basic teachings are summarized in the ancient statements of Christian belief, especially the Apostles' Creed, the Nicene Creed, the Athanasian Creed, and the Definition of Chalcedon.

THE APOSTLES' CREED

I believe in God, the Father almighty,
   Maker of heaven and earth.
And in Jesus Christ, his only Son, our Lord;
   Who was conceived by the Holy Spirit,
   and born of the Virgin Mary;
   Suffered under Pontius Pilate,
   Was crucified, died, and buried.
He descended into hell;
   On the third day he rose from the dead;
   He ascended into heaven and is seated
   at the right hand of the Father;
   From thence he will come to judge the living and the dead.
I believe in the Holy Spirit, the holy catholic church,
   The communion of saints, the forgiveness of sins,
   The resurrection of the body, and the life everlasting.

Main Branches

Roman Catholicism—worldwide church governed by the Pope (also called the Bishop of Rome) from the Holy See in Vatican City

Eastern Orthodoxy—national churches (Armenian, Greek, Russian, etc.) governed by local bishops under the leadership of patriarchs; the Ecumenical Patriarch of Constantinople (Istanbul, Turkey) has primacy of honor

Protestantism—no centralized organization or leadership; liturgical denominations include Lutheran, Anglican, and Presbyterian churches; non-liturgical denominations include Baptist, Congregational, and Pentecostal churches

JEHOVAH'S WITNESSES (WATCHTOWER BIBLE & TRACT SOCIETY)

KEY PERSON/FOUNDER, DATE, LOCATION

Charles Taze Russell (1852–1916), succeeded as president by Joseph F. Rutherford (1869–1942). Began 1879 in Pittsburgh, Pennsylvania. Headquarters in Warwick, New York.

Key Writings

All current Watchtower publications, including

- the Bible (*New World Translation* only)
- *What Can the Bible Teach Us?*
- *How to Remain in God's Love*
- The *Watchtower* and *Awake!* magazines

WHO IS GOD?

Witnesses believe in a one-person God, called Jehovah. No Trinity. Jesus is the first thing Jehovah created. Calling God by his personal name—"Jehovah"—is of utmost importance. God's true followers can be identified by their use of "Jehovah" in their prayers, congregational singing, preaching, and Bible study. (Many Witnesses believe that if "Jehovah" is not invoked in prayer, the prayer may go to some other "god.")

WHO IS JESUS?

Witnesses claim that Jesus is not God. Instead, the Father (Jehovah) and his Son (Jesus) are two separate "gods"—Jesus is an inferior "god" serving

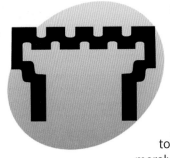

under Jehovah (who is the "only true God").

Before he lived on earth, Jesus was Michael, the archangel. He was the first one created, and Jehovah made the universe through him. When Jesus came to earth, he ceased to exist as Michael and became merely a perfect human. After Jesus died on a torture stake (not a cross), his human body was "disposed" of by God's power; he rose spiritually (not bodily) from the dead as the "resurrected Jesus Christ."

Since angels are invisible, Jesus fabricated physical bodies resembling his original body to convince his disciples that he had risen from the dead. Since 1914, when Jesus' "invisible presence" on earth began, he has been reigning from heaven, awaiting the battle of Armageddon in which he will rid the earth of human governments and set up "Paradise" under "Jehovah's Kingdom government arrangement."

Misunderstanding the Trinity

The Watchtower Society erroneously claims that the Christian doctrine of three persons in one God is a pagan concept comparable to the triadic "gods" of Babylonian and Egyptian mythology. It also argues that there is no basis in Scripture or ancient church history for the Trinity, and has mistranslated its version of the Bible to support its position.

WHO IS THE HOLY SPIRIT?

Witnesses believe the "holy spirit" is not God, but rather an impersonal, invisible, active force—the "energy" Jehovah projects to accomplish his will.

Apostasy and Restoration

Jehovah's Witnesses claim that Christianity fell into general apostasy (abandonment of the faith) under Emperor Constantine in the fourth century AD. God appointed Charles Taze Russell to restore pure worship in the last days and establish the Watchtower Society to provide spiritual truth through literature such as *The Watchtower* and *Awake!*

Charles Taze Russell

HOW TO BE SAVED

Be baptized as a Jehovah's Witness. Most followers must earn everlasting life on Earth by "door-to-door work." Salvation in heaven is limited to 144,000 "anointed ones"—a number that has already been reached.

More Salvation Requirements

Jesus died as a "ransom sacrifice" to buy back what Adam lost: the right to perfect life on earth. Most Witnesses hope to be found worthy enough to be "saved" from destruction in the future battle of Armageddon and to survive into God's new earthly system of rule, when "paradise" will be restored to Earth. The four requirements for salvation are:

- taking in knowledge of Jehovah God and of Jesus Christ
- obeying God's laws and conforming one's life to the moral requirements set out in the Bible

- belonging to and serving with God's one true channel and organization (the Watchtower Society)
- being loyal to God's organization

Salvation is earned through a combination of faith plus good works. True Christians can have no assurance of eternal life. They must work toward perfection throughout this life, and then throughout Christ's 1,000-year reign on earth. Next they must pass the final test of Satan (during which Satan is released from the pit to tempt all faithful Witnesses one last time) before God will grant them eternal life. If they fail at any point they risk annihilation (eternal destruction).

A Record of False Prophecy

Jesus predicts the coming of prophets who will mislead many by falsely announcing his return (Matthew 24:23–34). The Watchtower Society fulfills the criteria of a false prophet, having first pointed to 1874 as the date when Christ's invisible presence began and currently teaching that it began in 1914. It has repeatedly predicted the end of the age: 1914, 1915, 1918, 1925, 1940s, and 1975. While demanding absolute devotion to its teachings and proclaiming that it alone has "the Truth," the Watchtower has also reversed itself on a number of other doctrines.

OTHER FACTS, BELIEFS, OR PRACTICES

Also known as the International Bible Students Association. Witnesses meet in "Kingdom Halls" instead of churches. Active members ("publishers") proselytize door-to-door. Once a year members observe the Memorial of Jesus' death/Lord's Evening Meal (Communion); only "anointed ones" may partake. Witnesses are forbidden to vote, salute the flag, serve in the military, accept blood transfusions, or celebrate holidays and birthdays. They also reject the symbol of the cross.

No "Independent Thinking"

Spiritual truth is not given to God's people individually, but only through his ordained channel (the Watchtower Society). Thus, Jehovah's Witnesses must accept the Watchtower's interpretation of Scripture over their personal ideas and analyses; "independent thinking" is dangerous. Any Witness who challenges the Watchtower's current doctrines may be labeled prideful and "spiritually weak" and be subject to shunning by other Witnesses, including close family members.

Two Classes of Christians

According to the Watchtower Society, 144,000 people living between the day of Pentecost (c. AD 30) and 1935 were chosen by Jehovah to rule with him in heaven as spirits. They are called the "anointed class," the "little flock," or the "heavenly class." Since 1935, whenever members of the little flock fall away from the true faith, God replaces them with other Jehovah's Witnesses. All Jehovah's Witnesses after 1935 who are actively obeying Jehovah—along with those from all ages who never heard of Christ but were not wicked—are the "other sheep," or "great crowd." The great crowd will have a chance to live forever in paradise on Earth. The heavenly class and the great crowd will remain eternally separated; the "earthly class" will never see God or Christ.

New Covenant Privileges Only for the 144,000

The Watchtower says that only members of its heavenly class are parties to the new covenant. They alone have Jesus as their mediator, are "born again," have "adoption" as God's children, are members of the "Christian congregation" (the church), may partake of the "memorial emblems" of Jesus' last supper once a year, and will rule from heaven over the earth.

MORMONISM
(LATTER-DAY SAINTS)

KEY PERSON/FOUNDER, DATE, LOCATION

Joseph Smith, Jr. (1805–1844) organized what is now the Church of Jesus Christ of Latter-day Saints (LDS) in 1830 near Rochester, New York. Headquarters in Salt Lake City, Utah.

Joseph Smith, Jr.

WHO IS GOD?

No Trinity. God our Heavenly Father (also known as Elohim) was once a man, but "progressed" to godhood. He possesses a body of flesh and bone. The church teaches that "As man is, God once was; as God is, man may become." Thus worthy members can aspire to godhood themselves.

Misunderstanding the Trinity

Mormonism teaches that God the Father, Jesus Christ, and the Holy Ghost are three Gods, though united in purpose as the one "Godhead." This is not the same as the Christian doctrine of the Trinity, in which there is only one true God (Deuteronomy 6:4) existing eternally in three persons as the Father, Son, and Holy Spirit. Mormons also believe that in addition to a Heavenly Father, all humans and spirits have a Heavenly Mother—despite the fact that there is no mention of her in the Bible or any Mormon scripture.

WHO IS JESUS?

Jesus is a separate being from Heavenly Father. He was first brought forth as a spirit child by Heavenly Father and Mother in the pre-mortal realm. He is the "elder brother" of all men and spirit beings (including Lucifer). Jesus' mortal body was created through sexual union between Heavenly Father and Mary. Early Mormon leaders claimed that Jesus was married. His suffering in Gethsemane and death on the cross do not provide full atonement for all sin, but do provide everyone with resurrection.

WHO IS THE HOLY SPIRIT?

The Holy Spirit is the third member of the Mormon godhead but lacks a body of flesh and bones. He is frequently called the Holy Ghost, Spirit of the Lord, Spirit of God, and the Comforter. The "gift of the Holy Ghost" can only be given by a Mormon priesthood holder after an individual has been baptized into the Mormon church.

Apostasy and Restoration

According to Mormonism, after the death of Jesus' original apostles the Christian church gradually slipped into "the Great Apostasy"—a complete and universal abandonment of true Christian principles. Though no one knows exactly when this took place, Christian doctrine became thoroughly corrupted, and the priesthood authority necessary to administer key ordinances like baptism and the Lord's Supper (Communion) was lost.

Key Writings

- *Book of Mormon*
- *Doctrine and Covenants*
- *Pearl of Great Price*
- The Bible (considered far less reliable than the newer Mormon scriptures); the King James Version is used, together with excerpts from Joseph Smith's "Inspired" translation
- Authoritative teachings of Mormon prophets and other LDS "general authorities"
- *Ensign* and *Liahona* magazines

The restoration of true Christianity began when Heavenly Father and Jesus Christ appeared to a young Joseph Smith in the spring of 1820. In this "First Vision" Jesus told Smith that all the churches were wrong and that all their creeds (statements of belief) were an abomination. God used Smith to organize his true church again in 1830.

HOW TO BE SAVED

All who dwell on earth will eventually be resurrected by grace. Mormons who are exalted to godhood will be saved by grace *plus* works (which include faithfulness to church leaders, Mormon baptism, tithing, ordination, marriage, and secret temple rituals). No eternal life without Mormon membership.

More on Salvation

A life of obedience to God's commandments is necessary to have one's sins forgiven and receive "eternal life"—exaltation (and godhood)—in the celestial kingdom where Heavenly Father dwells. Thomas Monson of the LDS

First Presidency stated: "It is the celestial glory which we seek. It is in the presence of God we desire to dwell. It is a forever family in which we want membership. Such blessings must be earned."

The Book of Mormon teaches that the grace of Christ only takes effect after the Latter-day Saint has denied himself "of all ungodliness." Though both biblical Christianity and Mormonism have a concept of repentance, in Mormonism this involves successfully abandoning *all* sin. The *Gospel Principles* manual states: "Those who receive forgiveness and then repeat the sin are held accountable for their former sins." Sin that is not overcome robs the Mormon of any assurance of attaining eternal life in the celestial kingdom.

WHAT HAPPENS AFTER DEATH?
After the final judgment, nearly everyone goes to one of three separate heavenly "kingdoms" (telestial, terrestrial, and celestial), with some achieving godhood. The Devil and his angels, plus the "sons of perdition" (Mormons who left the church and fought it despite knowing it was true), will be condemned to "outer darkness."

OTHER FACTS, BELIEFS, OR PRACTICES
Secret temple "endowment" rituals and "celestial marriage" available only to members in good standing. Baptism on behalf of the dead. Tithing essential. "Word of Wisdom"

prohibits tobacco, alcohol, and "hot drinks" such as coffee and tea. Two-year missionary commitment for young males (one and a half years for females) is encouraged. Church welfare plan provides for needy members and promotes self-reliance. Extensive genealogical program. Males of African ancestry were denied access to Mormon priesthood and full temple privileges until 1978.

Polygamy

Once essential

Between 1852 and 1890 the practice of polygamy became essential for any Mormon hoping to achieve exaltation. Mormon prophet Brigham Young (1801–1877) proclaimed that the "only men who become Gods, even the Sons of God, are those who enter into polygamy."

Brigham Young

Still valid

Though it was necessary for Mormon leaders to formally renounce plural marriage in 1890, today Mormon widowers may be spiritually "sealed" for eternity to more than one wife. The churches teach that the principle of polygamy remains valid, and its earthly practice will resume after Jesus' Second Coming and the start of the millennium.

The Book of Mormon

Mormonism claims...

The Book of Mormon is a miraculous translation of an ancient document. By "the gift and power of God," Joseph Smith interpreted the "reformed Egyptian" characters on the golden plates that the angel Moroni gave him in 1827.

Artistic representation of the gold plates

The Book of Mormon gives an account of three people groups (the Lehites, Jaredites, and Mulekites) who migrated from the Middle East and inhabited the American continents between about 2000 BC and AD 400.

You should know...

The LDS church asserts that the Book of Mormon is an ancient document. However, unlike the Bible, the Book of Mormon is published without maps, and there is no archaeological evidence to support its unique historical claims. Further, its nineteenth-century origin is exposed by the way it quotes and paraphrases passages from the New Testament, and it mentions controversial issues (such as freemasonry and infant baptism) that were hotly disputed during Smith's lifetime.

MIND SCIENCES/ NEW THOUGHT

KEY PERSON/FOUNDER, DATE, LOCATION
No one founder. The best-known groups are Christian Science, founded by Mary Baker Eddy (1821–1910), headquarters Boston, Massachusetts; and Unity, founded by Charles (1854–1948) and Myrtle Fillmore (1845–1931), headquarters Unity Village, Missouri.

KEY WRITINGS
All groups were influenced by metaphysical author P. P. Quimby (1802–1866) and are essentially gnostic and pantheistic. Thus the Bible is considered limited and inferior, requiring spiritual interpretation through such works as

- *Science and Health with Key to the Scriptures* by Mary Baker Eddy (1875)
- *Lessons in Truth* by H. Emilie Cady (1896)
- *Metaphysical Bible Dictionary* by Charles Fillmore (1931)

WHO IS GOD?
Christian Science: God is "Father-Mother"—an impersonal Principle of life, truth, love, intelligence, and spirit. God is all that truly exists; matter is an illusion.

Unity: God is invisible, impersonal power—interchangeable with "Principle," "Law," "Being," "Mind," "Spirit." God is in everything, much as the soul is in the body. The spirit is reality; matter is not.

WHO IS JESUS?
Christian Science: Jesus was neither God nor Christ ("the divine idea"). He was not "the Way" to salvation, but the "Way-shower." Jesus did not die on the cross, did not

rise again physically, and will not return.

Unity: Jesus was neither the Christ nor God, but a man with "Christ Consciousness." Jesus lived many times and was in search of his own salvation. He did not die as a sacrifice for sin and was not bodily resurrected.

WHO IS THE HOLY SPIRIT?

Christian Science: "Holy spirit" is redefined as "Divine Science."

Unity: The Holy Spirit is the law of God in action, the "executive power of both Father and Son," a "definite" thought in the mind of man.

SALVATION AND THE AFTERLIFE

Christian Science: Man does not sin; sin, evil, sickness, and death are not real. Salvation is being "saved from error" through practicing Christian Science. Heaven and hell are states of mind. No reincarnation.

Unity: One realizes salvation by recognizing that each person is as much a Son of God as Jesus is. There is no evil, no devil, no sin, no poverty, and no old age. One is reincarnated until he learns these truths and becomes "perfect." No literal heaven or hell.

Other Facts, Beliefs, or Practices

Christian Scientists use "practitioners" (professional healers who "treat" supposed illnesses for a fee) instead of doctors. Healing comes by realizing one cannot *really* be sick or hurt and that the body cannot be ill, suffer pain, or die. Christian Science maintains thousands of public "reading rooms" for study and contemplation.

Unity is widely known for its Silent Unity "affirmative" prayer ministry and its *Daily Word* devotional. Unlike Christian Science, Unity promotes various eastern/occult authors and ideas.

BRANHAMISM

KEY PERSON/FOUNDER, DATE, LOCATION

The American faith healer and self-proclaimed prophet William Marrion Branham (1909–1965), "the messenger of the Laodicean Church Age" and "Elijah the Prophet."

Key Writings

The Bible (King James Version), which can only be properly understood through Branham. Heavy reliance on meticulously transcribed sermons and books authored by Branham, such as

- *An Exposition of the Seven Church Ages* (1965)

- *The Revelation of the Seven Seals* (1967)

- *Conduct, Order, Doctrine of the Church* (1973–74), 2 vols.

- *Footprints on the Sands of Time* (1975), 2 vols.

Branham's writings and audio sermons are translated and distributed worldwide by independent Branhamite groups, including Voice of God Recordings (USA) and Cloverdale Bibleway (Canada).

WHO IS GOD?

The Trinity is false, and Trinitarians believe in "three gods." Instead, God is one eternal and all-powerful being who "wasn't even God" before he made creatures to worship him.

JESUS AND THE HOLY SPIRIT

Branham's teachings on Jesus are confusing and often contradictory. He identified Jesus with the Holy Spirit (who came forth from God as the "Logos"). God created Jesus as a sinless human inside of Mary to provide a physical dwelling for the Holy

Spirit, who entered Jesus at his baptism and left him in the Garden of Gethsemane (because "He had to die a man"). Today Jesus inhabits believers as the Holy Spirit. Branham predicted that Jesus would return by 1977.

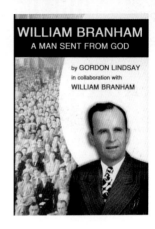

SALVATION AND THE AFTERLIFE

Jesus died for everyone. A person is saved when he or she has faith to be saved and accept Jesus as personal savior. The true evidence of someone having the Holy Spirit is recognizing Branham as the voice of God. Salvation can be lost by not accepting Jesus as savior, or by losing faith in one's salvation. At death, "Message believers" wait in the "sixth dimension" until Jesus' return. For now, unbelievers who die go somewhere between heaven and earth. Hell is not eternal; Satan and the wicked will suffer and then be annihilated.

Other Facts, Beliefs, or Practices

Branhamite churches use various names, often including the word "Tabernacle." Symbols include the eagle, the pyramid, and a 1950 photo in which a "pillar of fire" appears above Branham's head. The "Serpent's Seed" doctrine says the fall in the garden of Eden resulted from Eve having sex with the serpent (who was inhabited by Satan); because of Eve, womankind is the primary cause of sin in the world.

WORLD MISSION SOCIETY CHURCH OF GOD (WMSCOG)

KEY PERSON/FOUNDER, DATE, LOCATION

Founded by Ahnsahnghong, a.k.a. Ahn Sahng-hong (1918–1985), considered "our heavenly Father Christ Ahnsahnghong" and "Second Coming Christ." Current leaders are Zahng Gil-ja ("Heavenly Mother") and Kim Joo-cheol ("general pastor"). First established in 1964 as "Witnesses of Jesus Church of God." Headquarters and New Jerusalem Temple are located in Bundang, South Korea.

WHO ARE GOD, JESUS, AND THE HOLY SPIRIT?

While the WMSCOG claims to believe in "the Holy Trinity," it actually rejects the historic Christian doctrine. Instead, it teaches a form of the ancient heresy known as modalism. One of the WMSCOG websites states that "God plays three different roles in the Trinity, having three different names and appearances, while maintaining His nature of God in each role."

Thus, the site continues, "The name of God the Father is Jehovah and the name of God the Son is Jesus.... The name of the Holy Spirit is Ahnsahnghong."

What's more, the WMSCOG actually affirms *two* Gods, teaching that the Old Testament Hebrew word "Elohim" refers to both God the Father *and* a living

Key Writings

The Bible, plus seven "Truth Books" (six written by Ahnsahnghong, one by Kim Joo-cheol) and the monthly *Elohist* magazine. Distribution of WMSCOG "insider" publications is tightly controlled.

person they call "God the Mother"—a Korean woman named Zahng Gil-ja (b. 1943). She is revered as "Heavenly Jerusalem" and "the Bride of Christ."

SALVATION AND THE AFTERLIFE

Human beings first existed as "angels" in heaven, but as another WMSCOG site explains, "we committed treason against God...and were cast down to this earth." Requirements for salvation and eternal life include baptism, accepting "Heavenly Mother," keeping the Sabbath, and keeping the WMSCOG "New Covenant Passover." After death, one's soul "sleeps" until the resurrection and Judgment Day. The unsaved will go to hell, "a place of eternal torment"; the saved will again become "angels in heaven."

OTHER FACTS, BELIEFS, OR PRACTICES

- Ahnsahnghong's movement split in two after his death. The New Covenant Passover Church of God (NCPOG), in which his son Ahn Kwang-Sup is a leader, rejects the teaching that Ahnsahnghong is God and that there is a "Heavenly Mother."
- WMSCOG is considered "Zion" and "the only true church which God has established on this earth," while other denominations are shunned as "Babylon churches." Members reject the symbol of the cross, Christmas, and worshiping on Sunday as "pagan." Women must wear veils in worship.
- The group has faced repeated controversies over alleged end-of-the-world predictions for 1988, 1999, and 2012.

JUDAISM

KEY PERSON/FOUNDER, DATE, LOCATION
Abraham of the Bible, about 2000 BC, and Moses in the ancient Near East.

MAIN BRANCHES

- Orthodox
- Conservative
- Reform

KEY WRITINGS
- The Tanakh (Old Testament), especially the Torah (or Pentateuch)—the first five books of the Bible
- The Talmud (explanation of the Tanakh), consisting of the Mishnah and the Gemara
- Writings of sages, such as Maimonides (AD 1135?–1204)

WHO IS GOD?
God is spirit. To Orthodox Jews, God is personal, all-powerful, eternal, and compassionate. To other Jews, God is impersonal, unknowable, and can be defined in a number of ways. No Trinity.

WHO IS JESUS?
Jesus is seen either as an extremist false messiah or a good, but martyred Jewish *rabbi* (teacher). Many Jews do not consider Jesus at all. Jews (except Messianic Jews and Hebrew Christians) do not believe he was the Messiah, the Son of God, or that he rose from the dead. Orthodox Jews

believe that the Messiah will restore the Jewish kingdom and eventually rule the earth.

WHO IS THE HOLY SPIRIT?

Some believe the Holy Spirit is another name for God's activity on earth. Others say it is God's love or power.

HOW TO BE SAVED

Some Jews believe that prayer, repentance, and obeying the Law (*halakha*) are necessary for salvation. Others believe that salvation is the improvement of society.

WHAT HAPPENS AFTER DEATH?

There will be a physical resurrection. The obedient will live forever with God, and the unrighteous will suffer. Some Jews do not believe in a conscious life after death.

OTHER FACTS, BELIEFS, OR PRACTICES

Meeting in synagogues on the Sabbath, which takes place from sunset on Friday until nightfall on Saturday. Circumcision of males. Many Jews carefully observe dietary restrictions (*kosher* means "fit to eat" according to Jewish law), shunning pork and other "unclean" foods. Jerusalem is considered the holy city.

Major Celebrations

Include...

- *Passover*—commemorates the story of the Exodus in the Bible. Observed with a Seder, a ceremonial meal.

- *Rosh Hashanah* (Jewish New Year)—the first of the Jewish High Holy Days.

- *Yom Kippur* (Day of Atonement)—a most holy day of fasting and prayer.

- *Hanukkah* (Festival of Lights)—primarily a family celebration centered around lighting a nine-candled menorah.

27

KABBALAH CENTRE

KEY PERSON/FOUNDER, DATE, LOCATION

Shraga Feivel Gruberger (1927?–2013), now known as
Philip S. Berg. Followers claim
it was originally founded in
1922 by Rav Yehuda Ashlag
(1885–1954) in Jerusalem.
Headquarters in Los Angeles,
California.

KEY WRITINGS

- *The Zohar* ("Book of
  Splendor"), the Centre's
  23-volume translation of mystical Aramaic and Hebrew
  writings which first appeared in Spain in the 13th–14th
  centuries.
- Books by Philip Berg and his son,
  Yehuda, including
  - » *Kabbalah for the Layman*
    (1985–1988), 3 vols.
  - » *The Essential Zohar* (2002)
  - » *The 72 Names of God* (2004)

WHO IS GOD?

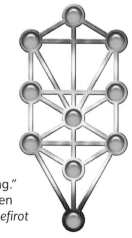

The supreme being (*Ein Sof*,
"endlessness") is unknowable,
infinite, and impersonal—described
as both "everything" and "in everything."
This Creator God is revealed through ten
emanations or manifestations, called *sefirot*

("numbers"), which are illustrated with male and female aspects as ten points on the Kabbalah "Tree of Life" diagram.

WHO IS JESUS?

Jesus is not God, nor is he the Jewish Messiah (who is yet to come). Some believe that Jesus was a Kabbalist himself.

WHO IS THE HOLY SPIRIT?

Ru'ah HaKodesh (Hebrew, "spirit of holiness") is said to be a state of the soul that enables one to prophesy.

HOW TO BE SAVED

Man is a vessel with the spark of the Creator; he repairs God/the universe by right living and sharing so he can hold more of the Creator's light. Kabbalah enables us to understand and live in harmony with spiritual laws on which the universe operates.

SALVATION AND THE AFTERLIFE

Followers believe in reincarnation, not resurrection. Man is said to climb the Tree of Life back to God, and thus return to Paradise and "restore Eden."

Other Facts, Beliefs, or Practices

Evil is not a moral issue, but a question of violating universal principles. Controversy over expensive merchandise, courses, and fundraising methods. Followers use the red string bracelet and other talismans to protect themselves from the "Evil Eye" and various negative spiritual influences. Extensive use of astrology and meditation.

ISLAM

KEY PERSON/FOUNDER, DATE, LOCATION

Founded in Mecca, Arabia by Muhammad (AD 570–632), considered the greatest man who ever lived and the last of more than 124,000 messengers sent by Allah (God). Main types: Sunni ("people of the tradition"), Shi'a ("party of Ali"), Sufi (mystics).

MAIN BRANCHES

Sunni: Four "schools of law" (*Madh'hab*)—Hanafi, Maliki, Hanbali, and Shafi'i

Shi'a: Three branches—majority "Twelvers" (*Jafari*), who believe in a succession of twelve infallible, divinely ordained imams; "Seveners" (*Ismaili*); and "Fivers" (*Zaidi*)

WHO IS GOD?

Allah is One and absolutely unique. He cannot be known. The greatest sin in Islam is *shirk*, or associating anything with Allah. Human qualities like fatherhood cannot be attributed to Allah. Based on the Qur'an, Muslims

Key Writings

The Holy Qur'an (Koran), revealed to Muhammad by the angel Gabriel. Essential commentaries are found in the *Sunnah* ("tradition"), composed of *Hadith* ("narrative") and *Sirah* ("journey"). Islam affirms that God sent books to Moses, David, and Jesus, but Jews and Christians have corrupted the original texts.

believe that Christians worship three gods—Allah, Jesus, and Mary—and are therefore guilty of *shirk*.

Sunni: Estimated 1.5 billion worldwide

Shi'a: Up to 200 million, primarily in Iran, Iraq, Lebanon, Azerbaijan, Bahrain

WHO IS JESUS?

Jesus (*Isa* in Arabic) was not God or the Son of God. His virgin birth is likened to Adam's creation. He was sinless, a worker of miracles (by Allah's permission only—not by his own initiative or power), and one of the most respected prophets sent by Allah. He was neither crucified nor resurrected. He, not Muhammad, will return to play a special role before the future judgment day, perhaps turning Christians to Islam.

WHO IS THE HOLY SPIRIT?

"Holy spirit" can refer to Allah, to the angel Gabriel, or to a spirit used by Allah to give life to man and inspire the prophets.

HOW TO BE SAVED

Humans are basically good—needing no atonement for sin or spiritual rebirth—but fallible and in need of guidance. The balance between good and bad deeds determines one's destiny in paradise or hell. Allah may tip the balances toward heaven. One should always live with the fear of Allah and judgment day.

WHAT HAPPENS AFTER DEATH?

Belief in bodily resurrection. One may pray for and seek favor for the dead before judgment day. Paradise includes a garden populated with *houris*, maidens designed by Allah to provide sexual pleasure to righteous men.

Eschatology

Sunni: Majority believe that a figure known as the *Mahdi* ("guided one"), from Muhammad's family, will appear with Jesus before the final judgment.

Shi'a: Majority believe in a series of twelve imams serving as Muhammad's spiritual and political successors. The final one, Muhammad al-Mahdi (b. AD 869), is alive but hidden (in "occultation") since AD 874; at the proper time he will appear with Jesus.

OTHER FACTS, BELIEFS, OR PRACTICES

Muslims meet in mosques for prayers, sermons, counsel. Emphasis on hospitality, developing a sense of community, and maintaining honor (or avoiding shame). *Shari'a*, actualized in different schools of *fiqh* (Islamic law),

governs all aspects of life in places where it is enforced. *Jihad* ("fight") may be used to refer either to one's inner struggle to obey God or to literal warfare.

Muslims who convert to Christianity or other religions face persecution and possible death according to common Islamic law, but such penalties are enforced differently from one majority-Muslim country to another.

Succession
Sunni: Muhammad's successors (called *caliphs*) should ideally be chosen by consensus/election. Only four were actually elected, beginning with Abu Bakr (c. AD 573–634). As of AD 661, caliphs came from a succession of three hereditary dynasties: the Umayyads, Abbasids, and Ottomans. There have been no new caliphs since 1924.

Shi'a: Muhammad's successors (called *imams*) should be from his family and descendants (*Ahl al-Bayt*). The first of these was his cousin and son-in-law, Ali (c. AD 600–661), and thereafter all imams were bloodline descendants from Fatimah (Muhammad's daughter and Ali's wife). No new imams since AD 869.

Major Celebrations

- *Eid al-Fitr* (Feast of Breaking the Fast) marks the end of Ramadan, the Islamic holy month of fasting (annual; dates vary)

- *Eid al-Adha* (Feast of the Sacrifice) commemorates Abraham's willingness to obey God's command to sacrifice his son, and marks the end of the annual pilgrimage to Mecca (annual; dates vary)

DEFINITIONS

Allah—the proper pre-Islamic Arabic name for God, used even today by Arabic-speaking Christians as well as by Muslims.

Hadith (Arabic, "account," "narrative")—thousands of reports of sayings or behaviors of Muhammad, which set a precedent for Muslim practice and became the basis of Sharia in most Islamic schools of law.

Isa Al Masih—"Jesus the Mes-si-ah." The Arabic word "Ma-sih" is similar to the Hebrew word. "Isa" for "Jesus" is an obscure version of the Arab Christians' *Yasu* (from Hebrew *Yeshua*).

Muslim—an Arabic term derived from the same root as the word for peace (*salam*). Note that the trilateral root _S_L_M_ is shared by all these related terms: SALAM, ISLAM, MUSLIM.

Sharia (Arabic, "path to water")—the ideal summary or essence of practical Islamic law (*fiqh*), based on the Sunna, Qur'an, and Hadith. Sharia is a guide to everyday life and salvation.

Shirk (Arabic, "associating")—idolatry or blasphemy; making others equal to God. An unpardonable sin, like disbelief (*qufr*).

Sufis—Muslim mystics who can be either Sunni or Shi'a, ranging from storytellers who seek to love Allah and his wisdom to those who induce trances through chanting the names of Allah or dancing (as by the widely known "whirling dervishes").

Main Teachings and Practices

SHI'A

Ten Ancillaries
- Prayers (*salat*)
- Fasting during Ramadan (*sawm*)
- Pilgrimage to Mecca (*hajj*)
- Almsgiving (*zakat*)
- One-Fifth Tax (*khums*)
- Religious War (*jihad*)
- Enjoining to Do Good (*amr-bil-ma'ruf*)
- Exhortation to Desist from Evil (*nahi-anil-munkar*)
- Loving the *Ahl al-Bayt* and their followers (*tawalla*)
- Disassociating from the Enemies of the *Ahl al-Bayt* (*tabarra*)

Five Principles
- Oneness (*tawhid*)
- Justice (*adl*)
- Prophethood (*nubuwwah*)
- Leadership (*imamah*)
- Day of Resurrection (*yawm al qiyyamah*)

SUNNI

Five Pillars (or duties)
- Profession of Faith (*shahadah*)
- Prayers (*salat*)
- Almsgiving (*zakat*)
- Fasting during Ramadan (*sawm*)
- Pilgrimage to Mecca (*hajj*)

Six Beliefs
- in Allah
- in Prophets and Messengers
- in Angels
- in Holy Books
- in the Day of Judgment and the Resurrection
- in the Decree (destiny/fate)

BAHÁ'Í FAITH

KEY PERSON/FOUNDER, DATE, LOCATION

Siyyid 'Alí-Muhammad, "the Báb" (1819–1850) and Mírzá Husayn-'Alí , "Bahá'u'lláh" (1817–1892). Founded 1844 in Iran. Headquarters in Haifa, Israel.

ميرزاح

Siyyid 'Alí-Muhammad

WHO IS GOD?

God is an unknowable divine being who has revealed himself through nine "manifestations" (prophets), including Adam, Moses, Krishna, Buddha, Jesus, Muhammad, and Bahá'u'lláh. No Trinity.

WHO IS JESUS?

Jesus is not God, nor is he the only way to God. Instead, Jesus is one of many manifestations of God. Each manifestation supersedes the previous one, giving new teachings about God. Jesus, who superseded Moses, was superseded by Muhammad, and most recently by the greatest, Bahá'u'lláh ("Glory of Allah"). Although Jesus died on the cross, he did not rise from the dead. The "Christ spirit" returned to earth in Bahá'u'lláh, who is superior to Jesus.

Greatest Name at the top of the Bahá'í House of Worship in Wilmette, Illinois

WHO IS THE HOLY SPIRIT?

Holy Spirit is divine energy from God that empowers every manifestation. "Spirit of Truth" refers to Bahá'u'lláh.

HOW TO BE SAVED

Faith in the manifestation of God (Bahá'u'lláh). Knowing and living by Bahá'u'lláh's principles and teachings.

WHAT HAPPENS AFTER DEATH?

Personal immortality based on good works, with rewards for the faithful. Heaven and hell are "allegories for nearness and remoteness from God," not actual places.

Key Writings

- Writings of Bahá'u'lláh and 'Abdu'l-Bahá, including
  - *Kitáb-i-Íqán* ("Book of Certitude") (1861)
  - *Kitáb-i-Aqdas* ("Most Holy Book") (1873)
- The Bible, interpreted spiritually to conform to Bahá'í theology

OTHER FACTS, BELIEFS, OR PRACTICES

Bahá'í originated as an Islamic sect and is severely persecuted in Iran. The Bahá'í faith teaches that all religions have the same source, principles, and aims. Stress on oneness and world unity. Regular local gatherings called "feasts." Local and national "spiritual assemblies" oversee administrative matters. The Universal House of Justice in Haifa, Israel, is the group's supreme legislative authority.

Universal House of Justice

NATION OF ISLAM

KEY PERSON/FOUNDER, DATE, LOCATION

Wallace D. Fard (1877?–1934?) in Detroit in 1930, but led
by Elijah Muhammad (1897–1975) beginning in 1934.
Louis Farrakhan (1933–) has led the movement since 1981.
Headquarters in Chicago, Illinois.

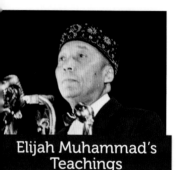

**Elijah Muhammad's
Teachings
about God**

- God is a black man.
- Millions of Allahs have lived and died since creation.
- Collectively the black race is God.
- Master Fard is the Supreme Allah & Savior.

KEY WRITINGS

Publicly, the Holy Qur'an is authoritative and the Bible is quoted often, but *Message to the Blackman in America (1965), Our Saviour Has Arrived (1974)*, and other books by Elijah Muhammad supply the group's distinctive views. Current teachings are promoted in *The Final Call* newspaper and speeches of Minister Farrakhan.

WHO IS GOD?

Officially, there is one God, Allah, as described in the Qur'an.

WHO IS JESUS?

Officially, Jesus is a sinless prophet of Allah. Privately, Jesus was born from adultery between Mary and Joseph, who was already married to another woman. Jesus was not crucified, but stabbed in the heart by a police officer. He is still buried in Jerusalem. Prophecies of Jesus' return refer to Master Fard, Elijah Muhammad, or to Louis Farrakhan.

WHO IS THE HOLY SPIRIT?
The Holy Spirit is not significant to this belief, but is generally regarded as the power of God or as the angel Gabriel who spoke to the prophet Muhammad.

HOW TO BE SAVED
People sin, but are not born sinful; salvation is through submission to Allah and good works. Older beliefs still held include: Fard is the savior; salvation comes from knowledge of self and realizing that the white race are devils who displaced the black race.

WHAT HAPPENS AFTER DEATH?
There is no consciousness or any spiritual existence after death. Heaven and hell are symbols. Statements about the resurrection refer to awakening "mentally dead" people by bringing them true teachings.

Other Facts, Beliefs, or Practices

Farrakhan's public messages coexist with earlier, more esoteric doctrines. Elijah Muhammad's older views (such as polytheism, God as the black race, Master Fard as Allah incarnate, white people as devils bred to cause harm) are still distributed, but public preaching now focuses on Islamic themes (one eternal God, non-racial emphasis) with frequent use of the Bible.

Eastern Religions: Fundamental Beliefs

There are important differences among the major eastern religions, and not all scholars agree on points of history and classification. Still, many foundational beliefs of eastern religious worldviews stand in stark contrast to the Christian worldview. To see how Christianity and eastern religions differ, it's helpful to understand basic concepts common to most eastern religions and New Age thought.

Pantheism is a bedrock of eastern religious philosophy. The meaning of the word comes from the Greek *pan* ("all") and *theos* ("God"). In pantheism, God is not separate from creation. "God" in pantheism is not a personal, loving creator as in Christianity, but a vague, impersonal force that exists in all things. Although some eastern religions incorporate devotion to gods or spirit beings, they do not believe in an all-powerful, loving God with whom anyone can have a personal relationship.

Reincarnation is a foundational belief in eastern religions, in which souls go through thousands of births, lives, and deaths.

Karma—"bad action" and attachment to the material world—is the negative agent that causes people to reincarnate. In early Hindu scriptures, reincarnation is described as smoke from a cremated soul rising into the clouds, where it falls back to the earth as rain that nourishes plants and animals in the food chain, eventually becoming human again. This is the opposite of the Christian belief that God creates us as individuals with one physical life on earth—in which we can accept or reject his loving gift of salvation—followed by a single resurrection.

Yoga and meditation are two of the main ways of attaining "salvation" in eastern religions. Salvation means escaping the countless painful cycles of reincarnation. Yoga and meditation are physical and mental practices developed as ways of reducing one's karma—the attachment to the physical world and to our individual selves. In Christianity, salvation is the free gift from God through his love and grace to anyone who will accept it; in eastern religions, salvation is something people constantly work to achieve by their own efforts.

HINDUISM

KEY PERSON/FOUNDER, DATE, LOCATION

No one founder. Began 1800–1000 BC in India. Majority of followers in India (80% of the population), with significant numbers in Nepal, Indonesia (Bali), South Africa, and the Caribbean.

MAIN BRANCHES

- **Shaivism**—emphasizes worship of the god Shiva; stresses the more radically impersonal nature of Brahman

Om, a sacred mantra syllable of Buddhism, Hinduism, Jainism, and Sikhism

- **Vaishnavism**—emphasizes the worship of Vishnu; understands Brahman in more personal manifestations (such as Krishna, hero of the Bhagavad Gita)
- **Shaktism**—emphasizes devotion to Shakti or the Devi (the divine mother) as the ultimate expression of the godhead

KEY WRITINGS

There are hundreds of Hindu scriptures. The most important collections are:

- the four *Vedas* ("knowledge") (c. 1500–1000 BC), the earliest texts

A manuscript illustration from the Mahabharata epic poem

42

- the *Brahmanas* (c. 900–500 BC), consisting mainly of rituals and mantras
- the *Upanishads* (c. 800–500 BC), 108 philosophical treatises
- the *Dharmashastras* (c. 100 BC–AD 200), ethical, civil, and criminal law (including the *Laws of Manu*)
- the *Brahma Sutras* (c. AD 100), 550 verses of cryptic descriptions on God, reality, salvation, and other matters
- the *Ramayana* (c. 500 BC) and the *Mahabharata* (c. 400 BC–AD 300), epic poems (the latter including the *Bhagavad Gita*)
- the *Puranas* (c. AD 400–1000), containing the "history of the universe"
- the *Tantras* (c. AD 300–1100), containing magical/occult rituals and spiritual exercises to accelerate enlightenment

WHO IS GOD?
God is "The Absolute," a universal spirit. Everyone is part of God (*Brahman*), but most people are not aware of it. Many Hindus worship gods and goddesses that are considered manifestations of Brahman.

God...and gods
Originally a religion of many gods (*polytheism*), Hinduism gradually developed into a philosophy known as *pantheism* (all is God)—see *Eastern Religions:*

Major Celebrations

- *Kumbh Mela* ("festival of the pot")— a triennial pilgrimage, rotating among four locations in India; the world's largest religious gathering

- *Diwali*—an annual festival of lights (October or November)

Fundamental Beliefs. Theistic and pantheistic views of God are taught by different schools of Hindu thought, and are often mingled.

In the non-theistic traditions, God is *not* a personal creator, distinct from his creation; instead, both the creature and its source are part of the same "big reality," called *Brahman-Atman*. Brahman is the Divine Totality, the ultimate reality, and Atman is the individual soul, like a spark from the huge fire of Brahman. As the twentieth-century Indian guru Muktananda said, "Worship your own inner self. God lives within you as you."

There are said to be as many as 33 million gods in Hinduism, and most Hindus worship one or more gods in spite of philosophical speculations about worshiping self. Shiva and Vishnu are monotheistic deities in some of the theistic Hindu traditions. Other popular deities include Kali/Durga/Shakti, Krishna, Rama, Ganesh, and Hanuman.

WHO IS JESUS?

Jesus Christ is considered a teacher, a guru, or an avatar (incarnation of the god Vishnu). He is a "son of God"—as are others. His death does not atone for sins, and he did not rise bodily from the dead.

WHAT HAPPENS AFTER DEATH?

Reincarnation into a better status (good karma) if a person has behaved well; if badly, a person can be reborn and pay for past sins (bad karma) by suffering.

HOW TO BE SAVED

Each human soul is destined to eventually merge with Brahman through thousands of reincarnations and much suffering. These life cycles, called *samsara* ("wandering"), refer to the soul's journey from one life to another until achieving *moksha* ("liberation"). In the non-theistic traditions, this liberation is nothing like "heaven."

One's final release from suffering and the cycles of reincarnation occurs when the soul dissolves into Brahman, like a raindrop falling into the ocean. Moksha amounts to the extinction of the individual personality; but in theistic Hindu traditions there is a concept of heaven as being present with God. Unlike Judaism and Christianity, Hinduism views history in terms of vast cycles of creation and destruction, including four eras known as *yugas*; this understanding permeates its doctrines and practices.

OTHER FACTS, BELIEFS, OR PRACTICES

- Hindus often use a mark called a *tilaka* on the forehead to represent the spiritual "third eye" (which is thought to be turned inward, toward God).

- In India, upper-caste Brahmin priests preside over rituals and ceremonies invoking various gods, which are often represented by elaborate idols; these rituals may serve both religious and cultural purposes.

- In India, the cow is protected as a sacred animal, though it is bred for its milk. Observant Hindus do not eat beef. Many maintain a largely vegetarian diet for the sake of compassion and nonviolence (*ahimsa*).

- Hinduism has no single unifying philosophy or tradition. It evolved over centuries as a mingling of historic religious influences that are not necessarily compatible with one another.

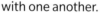

GURUS

Advanced spiritual seekers may become disciples of *gurus*, some of whom claim high spiritual attainment, even to the point that they will not be reincarnated because they have attained "enlightenment." "Guru and God are one" is a common expression.

The guru and his disciple have a relationship that is intimate and complex, creating a psychological and spiritual bond. During the disciple's initiation the guru may whisper a secret mantra into the disciple's ear, and the disciple may even surrender his will and personality to the guru. Widely known gurus include Sri Sri Ravi Shankar, Osho  (Bhagwan Shree Rajneesh), Maharishi Mahesh Yogi, Swami Muktananda, and Sathya Sai Baba.

DEFINITIONS

Ashram (Sanskrit, "abode," "residence")—a term often used for the retreat center of a guru.

Caste—a strict division of Indian society, based on differences of birth, which frequently determines one's status, profession, and occupation.

Mantra (Sanskrit, "thought form")—a word or phrase used repetitively in meditation to release the soul from bad karma and reincarnation.

Monism—the teaching that all reality is one. Advaita (non-dual) Vedanta is a major school of Hindu philosophy that teaches this, emphasizing that what we commonly call reality is contingent, an illusion that hides the true reality beyond our world.

Puja (Sanskrit, "worship")—includes food, flowers, and incense offerings accompanied by prayers and mantras.

HARE KRISHNA (ISKCON)

KEY PERSON/FOUNDER, DATE, LOCATION

A. C. Bhaktivedanta Swami Prabhupada (1896–1977)
began the International Society for Krishna Consciousness
(ISKCON) in 1966 in New York.
Based on sixteenth-century
Hindu teachings. Headquarters
in Mayapur, India.

KEY WRITINGS

- *Back to Godhead* magazine
- Prabhupada's translations
  of and commentaries on
  Hindu scriptures, especially
  - *Bhagavad-Gita as It Is*
    (1968)
  - *Srimad-Bhagavatam*
    (1978), 18 vols.

A. C. Bhaktivedanta
Swami Prabhupada

WHO IS GOD?

God is Lord Krishna. Krishna
is a personal creator; the souls of all living things are part of
him. Some practices that Krishna enjoys freely for his own
pleasure (such as intoxication and sex outside of marriage)
are prohibited to his devotees.

WHO IS JESUS?

Jesus is not important to ISKCON. He is usually considered an
enlightened vegetarian teacher who taught meditation. He is
not an incarnation of God. Some Krishna devotees consider

Jesus to be Krishna, while others say he is a great avatar (incarnation of Vishnu).

SALVATION AND THE AFTERLIFE

Indian scholar Vishal Mangalwadi explains that in ISKCON, "Man's problem is that he has forgotten his Krishna-consciousness and become entangled in this material world. He has to re-establish his link with Krishna and gain Krishna-consciousness. Only then will man get out of the cycle of births and deaths and live forever in *Goloka*" (heaven).

Other Facts, Beliefs, or Practices

ISKCON is known for practices such as *sankirtan* (includes publicly chanting the Hare Krishna "Maha Mantra" and book distribution), *japa yoga*, serving *prasadam* (ritually sanctified vegetarian food), and soliciting donations.

"Four regulative principles" require vegetarian diet, no intoxicants, no gambling, and sex for procreation only. New devotees are often attracted through feasts and Indian cultural programs; those who convert are given new names and may cut family ties.

Priest distributing prasadam

TRANSCENDENTAL MEDITATION (TM)

KEY PERSON/FOUNDER, DATE, LOCATION

Maharishi Mahesh Yogi (1918?–2008). Founded 1955–1958 in India, based on Hinduism and karma yoga. Headquarters in Vlodrop, the Netherlands.

Maharishi Mahesh Yogi

WHO IS GOD?

Each part of creation makes up "God" (Brahman). The Supreme Being is not personal. All creation is divine—"all is one."

WHO IS JESUS?

Jesus is not uniquely God. Like all persons, Jesus had a divine essence; unlike most, he discovered it. Christ didn't suffer and couldn't suffer for people's sins.

HOW TO BE SAVED

Humans have forgotten their inner divinity. Salvation consists of doing good in excess of evil in order to evolve to the highest state (final union of the self with Brahman) through reincarnation.

SALVATION AND THE AFTERLIFE

Reincarnation is based on karma (reaping the consequences of one's actions) until loss of self into union with Brahman. No heaven or hell.

OTHER FACTS, BELIEFS, OR PRACTICES

TM reportedly costs the average person almost $1,000 to learn. The initiation ritual requires veneration and an offering of flowers, fruit, and cloth before a picture of Maharishi's dead teacher, Guru Dev. TM is commonly practiced for 20 minutes twice a day by mentally repeating a mantra while sitting silently with one's eyes closed.

Other TM-related practices include astrology, use of crystals, and Maharishi Vedic Medicine. Maharishi University of Management in Iowa offers advanced TM programs in "Yogic Flying" (levitation) and "invisibility." Efforts to introduce TM in US public schools resulted in precedent-setting court decisions in 1977 and 1979 determining that TM is religious in nature.

Key Writings

- Hindu scriptures including the *Bhagavad-Gita*
- Maharishi Mahesh Yogi's writings, including
  - *Science of Being and Art of Living* (1963)
  - *Transcendental Meditation with Questions and Answers* (1967)

Transcendental Meditation headquarters
in Vlodrop, the Netherlands

SIKHISM

KEY PERSON/FOUNDER, DATE, LOCATION
Guru Nanak Dev Ji (1469–1539), in what is now the province of Punjab in Pakistan. Nine gurus followed (1504–1708). Main place of worship is the Golden Temple in Amritsar, India.

KEY WRITINGS
- Main scripture is the *Sri Guru Granth Sahib* ("the master book," also called *Adi Granth*), first compiled in AD 1604. It is worshiped by Sikhs, who consider it their final and perpetual guru.
- Other key works include
  - *Dasam Granth*
  - *Varan Bhai Gurdas*
  - *Sikh Reht Maryada*

WHO IS GOD?
One omnipresent god (referred to as *Waheguru*, "Wondrous Teacher"), who is known to the spiritually "awakened" only through meditation. Sikhism is also pantheistic, considering the universe itself part of God

Guru Nanak Dev Ji

(leaving no clear distinction between the Creator and creation). Representing God by pictures or idols is forbidden.

WHO IS JESUS?
Jesus is not specifically part of this belief, although the *Adi Granth* specifically denies the Trinity and describes God as "beyond birth" and incarnation.

HOW TO BE SAVED

Bondage to the material realm and the "five evils" (ego, anger, greed, attachment, and lust) condemn the soul to 8.4 million reincarnations. Those who successfully overcome these evils through proper behavior and devotion will be released from karma and the cycle of rebirth (*samsara*).

WHAT HAPPENS AFTER DEATH?

Upon death, those who escape samsara will be absorbed into God and lose their individuality, like a raindrop falling into the ocean. The *Adi Granth* both affirms and denies existence of a literal heaven and hell.

OTHER FACTS, BELIEFS, OR PRACTICES

Baptized (*Khalsa*) Sikhs are known by their use of the "five K's":

- the *kirpan* (a small ceremonial sword)
- *kes* (uncut hair)
- *kanga* (a small wooden comb)
- *kachera* (knee-length shorts)
- *kara* (steel bracelet)

Adult males wear a turban and include "Singh" in their names. Emphasis on full equality of men and women. Meeting places called *gurdwaras*, where a community kitchen serves free vegetarian food to all visitors.

BUDDHISM

KEY PERSON/FOUNDER, DATE, LOCATION

Gautama Siddhartha (563–483 BC), also known as Buddha (Pali, "enlightened one"). Founded in what is now Nepal and India as a reformation of Hinduism.

Buddha

Siddhartha was born into a ruling clan, and led a life of ease in which he was protected from all knowledge of human misery. When he subsequently encountered an old man, a sick man, and a decaying corpse, the shock sent him into a search to find a solution to life's suffering. He went on a pilgrimage of inquiry and meditation, but grew frustrated with the Hindu teachers he found.

One day while sitting under a Bodhi tree in northern India, he suddenly experienced "enlightenment" or "awakening," realizing that souls have the illusion of being reincarnated and floating through eternity, bound in ignorance, and suffering senselessly in one body after another.

MAIN BRANCHES

- **Theravada** ("path of the elders," also called Hinayana, or "lesser vehicle")— emphasizes *samadhi* ("concentration") meditation and *vipassana* ("insight") meditation

- **Mahayana** ("greater vehicle")—stresses that the essential Buddha-nature can be attained by all persons through meditation and the aid of *bodhisattvas* (enlightened beings who return to earth to aid Buddhists in spiritual need)

- **Vajrayana** ("diamond vehicle")—combines Mahayana, Indian *tantra*, and the occultic Bön religion of ancient Tibet

The *vajra* is the central symbol and an important ritual object in Vajrayana Buddhism

WHO IS GOD?

Buddha himself did not believe in the existence of God. Others speak of the Buddha as a universal enlightened consciousness or as a god.

Atheistic Religion

Buddhism is often considered a kind of "atheistic religion." Central to Buddha's teachings is the idea that pursuing or knowing "God" is irrelevant and can even interfere with one's quest for enlightenment. Buddha considered the Hindu gods as beings who are under the power of karma and who need to become human, convert

Key Writings

- The *Mahavastu* ("Great Story"), a collection covering Buddha's life story

- The *Jataka Tales*, 550 stories of the former lives of Buddha

- The Pali Canon or *Tripitaka* ("Three Baskets"), an oral tradition of the life and sayings of Buddha

- The *Tantras*, as recorded in Tibetan Buddhism

to Buddhism, and achieve spiritual awakening. Buddha considered it his mission to guide souls through the web of suffering and ignorance into salvation (*nirvana*).

WHO IS JESUS?
Jesus Christ is not part of the historic Buddhist worldview. Buddhists in the West today generally view Jesus as an enlightened teacher, while Buddhists in Asia believe Jesus is an *avatar* or a *bodhisattva*, but not God.

WHO IS THE HOLY SPIRIT?
The Holy Spirit is not part of this belief. However, Buddhists do believe in spirits, and some practice deity yoga and invite spirit possession.

WHAT HAPPENS AFTER DEATH?
Buddhists widely believe that, depending on one's karma, upon death one may go to one of six distinct spiritual planes: three "fortunate realms" (those of demigods, gods, and humans) and three "unfortunate realms" (those of animals, hungry ghosts, and "hell beings").

HOW TO BE SAVED
The religious lives of individual Buddhists vary greatly, as do their views on salvation. Some

Major Celebrations

- *Uposatha*, four monthly holy days

- *Vesak*, an annual commemoration of Buddha's birthday (May/June)

- *Vassa*, an annual rainy-season retreat (July–October)

- *Ullambana* (All Souls Day, or Hungry Ghost Festival), emphasizing veneration of ancestors (August)

strive for deliverance from their personal cravings through obedience to the Buddha's Noble Eightfold Path; others follow the teachings of a Buddhist master in order to achieve enlightenment; still others hope to enter a paradise by placing their faith in the merits of a compassionate Buddha or bodhisattva.

Noble Eightfold Path

- Right Understanding
- Right Thoughts
- Right Speech
- Right Action
- Right Livelihood
- Right Endeavor
- Right Mindfulness
- Right Concentration

However the Buddhist may seek it, one's ultimate deliverance is the same for all Buddhists: They believe that salvation is achieved by one's own virtuous works and by attaining the state of nothingness known as *nirvana*—that is, a permanent end to rebirths and suffering.

OTHER PRACTICES AND BELIEFS

- The five *silas* of moral conduct require Buddhists to refrain from killing, theft, sexual misconduct, lying or evil speech, and using illicit drugs and liquor.
- Zen Buddhism rejects theoretical knowledge and sacred writings in favor of experiencing sudden enlightenment through intensive seated meditation.

- Some Buddhist groups talk about an "eternal Buddha" (life-force).

- Some Mahayana Buddhist schools venerate enlightened spirits through demonstrations of respect, meditation, and gift-giving.
- Through the "Doctrine of Assimilation" the belief systems of other religions are blended into their form of Buddhism.

DEFINITIONS

Bodhisattva (Sanskrit, "enlightened existence," "awakened being")—in Mahayana Buddhism, one who has achieved enlightenment (Buddhahood) but delays ultimate release (nirvana) in order to first alleviate the suffering of others by his (or her) own merits. One of the most popular bodhisattvas is Avalokiteshvara, also known in China as the goddess of mercy Guanyin (or Kwan Yin) and in Japan as Kannon.

Dharma (Sanskrit, "that which upholds and supports")—refers to the order which makes the complexity of the natural and spiritual worlds possible. Dharma is a central concept in Indian civilization, both Hindu and

Buddhist, where it governs ideas about the proper conduct of living. It is symbolized by a wheel, seen in the center of the national flag of India.

Lama—the Tibetan Buddhist equivalent of the Hindu word "guru"; commonly translated to mean "spiritual teacher."

Skandha (Sanskrit, "heap")—one of the five identifying elements or "aggregates" that constitute the human individual. They disperse at one's death and then re-form at one's physical rebirth. They are form, feelings, perceptions, thought processes, and consciousness.

Four Noble Truths

Buddha taught that there are "Four Noble Truths," namely:

1. The reality of suffering

2. The cause of suffering (craving/desire)

3. The cessation of suffering (nirvana)

4. The "middle way"—following the Noble Eightfold Path

Tantra (Sanskrit, "loom," "warp")—the Tantras are the main scriptures of Vajrayana Buddhism. Tibetan tantrism is known for its emphasis on secrecy, magic, guru devotion, and sexual yoga.

The Dalai Lama

TENZIN GYATSO (1935–), the 14th Dalai Lama ("ocean of wisdom"), was born in rural Tibet. A monk of the Gelug ("Yellow Hat") sect of Tibetan Buddhism, he is said to be

the reincarnation of the previous thirteen Dalai Lamas, the god-kings of Tibet. In 1959, he fled Tibet because of conflict with the ruling Chinese, and now heads the Tibetan government in exile in Dharamsala, India. The Dalai Lama has done far more than anyone else to popularize Tibetan Buddhism in the West.

But there's more to the story. In 2001 the Dalai Lama told an interviewer for *Christianity Today*

Dalai Lama in Prague, 2016
Nadezda Murmakova/Shutterstock.com

that "Jesus Christ also lived previous lives," adding that Jesus "reached a high state, either as a Bodhisattva, or an enlightened person, through Buddhist practice or something like that."

Few people realize that the Dalai Lama's religion is also deeply occultic, thanks in part to the influence of the ancient Bön religion. The Dalai Lama consults the spirit-possessed Nechung Oracle for state decisions, and the Tantrism of Tibetan Buddhism includes the ritual use of human remains and of bodily excretions known as the "five ambrosias."

Family Tree of Far Eastern Religions

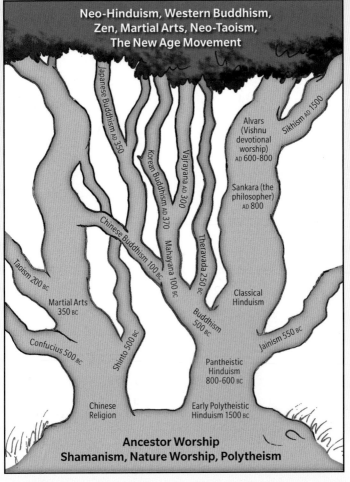

Neo-Hinduism, Western Buddhism,
Zen, Martial Arts, Neo-Taoism,
The New Age Movement

Japanese Buddhism AD 350

Korean Buddhism AD 370

Vajrayana AD 300

Alvars
(Vishnu
devotional
worship)
AD 600-800

Sikhism AD 1500

Sankara (the
philosopher)
AD 800

Chinese Buddhism 100 BC

Mahayana 100 BC

Theravada 250 BC

Taoism 200 BC

Martial Arts
350 BC

Classical
Hinduism

Confucius 500 BC

Shinto 500 BC

Buddhism
500 BC

Jainism 550 BC

Chinese
Religion

Pantheistic
Hinduism
800-600 BC

Early Polytheistic
Hinduism 1500 BC

Ancestor Worship
Shamanism, Nature Worship, Polytheism

SHINTO

KEY PERSON/FOUNDER, DATE, LOCATION

No founder. Shinto creation legends tell of native deities, called *kami*, who formed the islands of Japan. "Shinto" comes from the Chinese *shin tao* ("the way of the gods"). Native Japanese animist religion dating to 500 BC or earlier.

WHO IS GOD?

God is regarded not as personal creator, but as the force behind all the kami spirits. All of nature is animated by the kami—including things such as rocks, trees, or streams—making Shinto a combination of polytheism and pantheism. There are more than a dozen major kami, including *Amaterasu*, the sun goddess (represented in the rising sun of Japan's national flag), from whom the emperors of Japan descended.

PURPOSE OF LIFE/SALVATION

The main purpose of human existence is to lead an ethical life.

WHAT HAPPENS AFTER DEATH?

Each person continues existence as a kami.

Shimenawa, rope used to ward off evil spirits

OTHER FACTS, BELIEFS, OR PRACTICES

Nearly all followers are Japanese; very few non-Japanese convert. Japan's current emperor, Akihito (son of Hirohito, who ruled during World War II), is still regarded as divine by some Japanese.

Emperor Hirohito

The kami are worshiped in Japan's many shrines presided over by Shinto priests. Each shrine is dedicated to a specific kami who is said to respond to sincere prayers of the faithful. Prayers to the kami are offered for all of life's difficulties and blessings. Shinto recognizes many sacred places: mountains, springs, and significant historical locations.

Key Writings

Numerous texts dating from the eighth century AD and later. The four most important texts are:

- the *Kojiki* (AD 712), and *Nihon Shoki* (AD 720), two of Japan's national epics

- the *Rikkokushi* ("six national histories"), which includes

  » the *Shoku Nihongi* (AD 697–791)
  » the *Jinno Shotoki* (AD 1338–1341), a treatise on Japanese politics and history

CONFICIANISM

KEY PERSON/FOUNDER, DATE, LOCATION

Confucius or Kong Zi (551–479 BC), perhaps the most revered and influential figure in Chinese history, in China during the sixth century BC.

KEY WRITINGS

The "Four Books" of the Confucian canon are:

- The *Analects of Confucius* (c. 479–221 BC), compiled by his disciples shortly after his death
- The *Great Learning*, attributed to Confucius and Zengzi (505–436 BC)
- The *Doctrine of the Mean* by Zisi (481–402 BC)
- The *Book of Mencius*, attributed to the author of the same name

Other important writings include:

- The *Book of Filial Piety* (c. 400 BC)
- The "Five Classics," a collection which includes the *Classic of Changes* or *I Ching* (c. 1150 BC), a system of divination

WHO IS GOD?

Not everyone considers Confucianism an actual religion, and Confucius did not speak of God or gods. Despite this, he and nearly 200 disciples and sages are now worshiped in Confucian temples.

PURPOSE OF LIFE/SALVATION

While he did uphold the Chinese concept of "Heaven" as a spiritual reality, Confucius was a humanist concerned with ethical behavior in government and relationships. His ideal was the harmony of the perfected individual within a well-ordered society. His teachings can be summed up as

I Ching divination

"ethical humanism." He taught that the truly superior man is motivated by righteousness instead of profit.

SALVATION AND THE AFTERLIFE

Confucius did not speak of an afterlife or the soul, but he supported the ancient Chinese practice of ancestor worship—though more as an ethical system of respect for the dead.

Other Facts, Beliefs, or Practices

Include an emphasis on cultivating "filial piety" (a love and respect for one's parents and ancestors) and adhering to the laws of nature. Rituals include offerings to the spirits of ancestors, as well as observances to mark important stages of life (such as births, weddings, and funerals).

A "New Confucian" movement began in the twentieth century, reflecting the Neo-Confucian movement of AD 960–1279 that reveres Confucius, Buddha, and Laozi. Besides mainland China, Confucianism has had a significant influence on the cultures of Taiwan, Japan, Korea, and Vietnam.

TAOISM (DAOISM)

KEY PERSON/FOUNDER, DATE, LOCATION

Laozi ("the old man"), also called Lao-Tzu (c. 600–530 BC), said to be a contemporary of Confucius (though his true identity and historicity are in doubt). Tao ("the way") began in China in the sixth century BC, reaching near-final form by the second century BC. Adopted as a state religion by AD 440.

WHO IS GOD?

Taoism is polytheistic, with worship of deities such as the Jade Emperor. Laozi himself came to be venerated as a deity, along with many other "immortals."

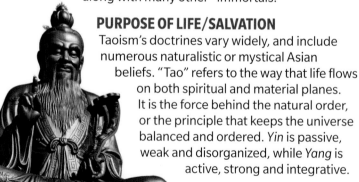

PURPOSE OF LIFE/SALVATION

Taoism's doctrines vary widely, and include numerous naturalistic or mystical Asian beliefs. "Tao" refers to the way that life flows on both spiritual and material planes. It is the force behind the natural order, or the principle that keeps the universe balanced and ordered. *Yin* is passive, weak and disorganized, while *Yang* is active, strong and integrative.

The Yin and Yang can be harmonized through

meditations and practices called *Wu wei* ("not doing"). The goal of Wu wei is alignment with Tao, revealing the smooth, invisible power within all things. Salvation is a vague concept in Taoism.

WHAT HAPPENS AFTER DEATH?

Some Taoists believe in reincarnation, while others believe life after death is a continuation of life on earth upheld by ancestor worship.

OTHER FACTS, BELIEFS, OR PRACTICES

Other beliefs include an emphasis on "five precepts" of interpersonal ethics, much like the five *silas* of Buddhism. Occult practices include spirit possession, mediumship, and divination. Taoism has also influenced Chinese martial arts (such as *Tai chi chuan*), traditional medicine, and *qigong*. Most followers are in China, although influence continues to grow steadily in North America.

Key Writings

- *Tao Te Ching* (4th century BC), ascribed to Laozi

- *Zhuangzi* (476–221 BC), ascribed to the author of the same name

- The much larger compilation of all Taoist works is the *Tao-tsang* ("Treasury of Tao"), collected around AD 400

Bagua, eight symbols used in Taoist cosmology

THE "NEW AGE" AND TODAY'S POP SPIRITUALITY

From the late 1960s until the late 1980s, the "New Age movement" swept through Western society. It popularized and repackaged a profusion of eastern mystical and occult beliefs and practices from centuries past, anticipating a revolution in consciousness that would usher in the "Age of Aquarius." As millions of today's spiritual consumers engage in a similar quest for healing, empowerment, success, and peace, they're crossing boundaries into dangerous territory.

A SPIRITUAL SUPERMARKET

Sociologist Carmen Kuhling describes New Age spirituality as "an eclectic mix of eastern mysticism, self-help therapy, paganism, and other philosophies." According to anthropologist Susan Love Brown, four of its main emphases are experience as the source of knowledge; ritual; healing oneself (whether spiritually or physically); and harmony among body, mind, and soul.

Popular authors like Deepak Chopra, Eckhart Tolle, and Rhonda Byrne (*The*

Secret) draw heavily from eastern religions (Buddhism, Hinduism) and New Thought, though they sometimes misquote the Bible to make their teachings more palatable. Some of their main—and most problematic—claims:

- Every human being is essentially divine (pantheism/monism—God is all).
- Jesus is not the only way; there are many paths to the truth about God.
- What I desire determines what happens in my life (law of attraction).
- God's Word (the Bible) is not our final authority.

SPIRITUALISM: FORERUNNER OF NEW AGE "CHANNELING"

This ancient belief was first widely popularized in the United States in 1848 by sisters Kate and Margaretta Fox of Hydesville, New York. Mediums conduct séances to allegedly contact and transmit messages from the dead. Spiritualists often use Ouija boards, crystal balls, and other instruments of divination. Today's "channelers" also claim to be the mouthpieces of spirits, but avoid physical "demonstrations" (such as levitating objects) used by nineteenth-century mediums.

DEFINITIONS

Ideas, expressions, and practices widely associated with popular spirituality

Altered state—a mental state in which critical thinking is suspended; produced by certain types of meditation, chanting, repetitive movements, or drugs; similar to a trance or light hypnotic state.

Aura—an energy field believed to surround a person's body with different colors revealing the spiritual, psychological, and physical states of the person.

Astrology (from the Greek *astrología*, "telling of the stars")—a form of divination that interprets the positions of the sun, moon, and planets as meaningful representations of a person's life, of an event, or of any entity that has a founding date (such as a country). Astrology differs from astronomy, which is the scientific study of space and heavenly bodies.

Channeling—allowing a spirit (demon) to speak through you; also called mediumism.

Chi (Qi)—from Taoism— believed to be a universal life energy permeating the universe and a person's body and manipulated for healing and spiritual benefits. Used in Feng Shui, acupuncture, and some martial arts.

Demon—a fallen angel who serves Satan. Can impersonate dead persons (such as ghosts) and other spirit beings.

Divination—reading hidden meanings in natural objects and/or receiving information about one's past, present, or future through supernatural means. Examples: astrology; numerology (arithmancy); reading cards (cartomancy), palms (chiromancy), glass or still water surfaces such as a crystal, mirror, or lake (scrying), tea leaves (tasseomancy), hexagram patterns (I Ching) or special Norse symbols (runes), and the earth to determine the best location for structures (geomancy).

Gnosticism (from the Greek *ginosko*, "I have knowledge")—a sect that emerged within or parallel to the Christian movement in the first and second centuries AD. Gnostics claimed to possess secret knowledge about God that was unavailable to others. Today's "God-consciousness" is similar to the insights and experiences that early Gnostics identified as *gnosis*.

Law of attraction—the belief that thoughts are "magnetic" and "have a frequency," and that by concentrating one's attention on certain desires for prolonged periods of time, one can gain anything one wants. This can work both positively (to attract prosperity) and negatively (to attract misfortune).

Magic(k)—to bend reality to one's will by using supernatural or mysterious powers. (Not to be confused with stage magic practiced by illusionists for entertainment.)

Medium—a psychic who attempts to communicate with the dead and/or other spirit beings.

Mindfulness—a mental state of awareness, actively focusing on one's present thoughts, feelings, bodily sensations, and surrounding environment in order to attain a sense of calm;

can be produced by meditation or other training.

Necromancy—a form of divination in which one seeks to communicate with the spirits of the dead. (From the Greek *nekrós*, "dead," and *manteía*, "divination.")

May also be used to refer to witchcraft or black magic in general.

Neopaganism—an umbrella term covering modern witchcraft/Wicca, Druidry, Ásatrú, Odinism, Native American shamanism, and related movements. Rituals, techniques, beliefs, and purposes can vary widely. Other terms include "the Craft" and "Earth Religions."

Occult—practices employed to uncover hidden meanings, wield supernatural powers, or contact spirits. (From the Latin *occulere*, "to conceal.")

Ouija® board—popular "talking board," a device manufactured by Hasbro, Inc. and widely used in necromancy and divination. Often promoted as a fun children's game, Ouija® boards can be a doorway to the occult.

Psychic—a person who receives information through spirits, or through paranormal powers of seeing (clairvoyance) or hearing (clairaudience).

Séance—a gathering in which people attempt to receive messages from the dead via a spirit medium.

Shamanism—belief that the world is filled with a variety of good and evil spirits (or forces) that can be ritually influenced or controlled by a *shaman* (a specially initiated intermediary), often by entering a trance state.

Spirit guide—a discarnate supernatural entity that acts as one's guide/companion; commonly a demon impersonating a ghost, angel, fairy, mermaid, animal, or extraterrestrial being. Thought to aid in divination or magic. Also called a "familiar."

The Real "Secret"

Human beings come equipped with a spiritual longing, a thirst for something beyond themselves. In reality, we long for the relationship with God for which we were created. "He has also set eternity in the human heart; yet no one can fathom what God has done from beginning to end" (Ecclesiastes 3:11). Ultimately, this longing is meant to guide humanity toward God himself.

Pop spirituality seems to offer the secret to relieving our fears, desires, and dreams. It promises control over the chaos of life—a formula for prosperity and wholeness. The good news: God is both the "secret" *and* the answer for which our souls are seeking, and he has revealed his identity in Jesus Christ, "in whom are hidden all the treasures of wisdom and knowledge" (Colossians 2:3).

SCIENTOLOGY

KEY PERSON/FOUNDER, DATE, LOCATION
Founded by L. Ron Hubbard (1911–1986) in 1954 in California. Major headquarters facilities in California and Florida.

WHO IS GOD?
Scientology does not define God or a Supreme Being, but rejects the Bible's description of God. Every person is a "thetan"—an immortal spirit with unlimited powers over its own universe—but not all are aware of this.

L. Ron Hubbard

WHO IS JESUS?
Jesus is rarely mentioned in Scientology. Jesus was not the Creator, nor was he an "operating thetan" (in control of supernatural powers, cleared from mental defects). Jesus did not die for anyone's sins. Scientology's symbolic use of the cross has no relation to Christianity.

HOW TO BE SAVED
No sin or need to repent. Salvation is freedom from reincarnation. One must work with an "auditor" on his "engrams" (negative experience units) to achieve the state of "clear." One then progresses up

E-meter, used to measure engrams

- *Dianetics: The Modern Science of Mental Health* (1952)

- *Scientology: The Fundamentals of Thought* (1971)

- *The Way to Happiness* (1980)

- Other works by Hubbard

the "bridge to total freedom" to higher "Operating Thetan" states and eventual control over matter, energy, space, and time (MEST).

WHAT HAPPENS AFTER DEATH?
Hell is a myth, and heaven is a "false dream."

OTHER FACTS, BELIEFS, OR PRACTICES
Members celebrate the birth of Hubbard and the anniversary of the publication of *Dianetics*. Controversy follows the group worldwide; numerous media outlets have produced damaging exposés. Organizations related to Scientology include Narconon, Criminon, Way to Happiness Foundation, WISE, Hubbard College of Administration, and Applied Scholastics.

ECKANKAR

KEY PERSON/FOUNDER, DATE, LOCATION

Founded in San Diego, California by Paul Twitchell (1908–1971) in 1965. Proclaims itself the "Religion of the Light and Sound of God" and "the Ancient Science of Soul Travel." Headquarters in Chanhassen, Minnesota. Currently led by Sri Harold Klemp (1942–), the "Mahanta" or "Living ECK Master."

WHO IS GOD?

God is a formless essence consisting of light and sound, called the *Sugmad* (said to be "neither masculine nor feminine" and "the source of all life"). The light and sound flow out of the Sugmad and return to it in a current called the *ECK*. Christianity is acknowledged as "an alternate path" to "a degree of enlightenment." The biblical concept of the Trinity is not recognized by Eckankar.

WHO IS JESUS?

Twitchell taught that the Devil "is the Jehovah of the Jewish faith and the Father of the Christian teachings.... Therefore we really see Jesus as a son of Kal Niranjan"—that is, the Devil. (Elsewhere the group teaches

Key Writings

- *The Shariyat-Ki-Sugmad* (1970)—considered "sacred scripture"

- Other books by Paul Twitchell, including

  » *The Tiger's Fang* (1967)
  » *Eckankar: The Key to Secret Worlds* (1969)
  » *The Flute of God* (1970)

- Writings by Harold Klemp

that Jesus was "the ECK Master in Judea.")

WHO IS THE HOLY SPIRIT?

"Holy Spirit" is used as another name for the "ECK" current.

HOW TO BE SAVED

Enlightenment, or union with the Sugmad, is attained by tuning in to the ECK current through "soul travel" and following it as it returns to its source.

WHAT HAPPENS AFTER DEATH?

After death one is reincarnated, repeatedly, until one returns to the Sugmad.

OTHER FACTS, BELIEFS, OR PRACTICES

Eckankar's practice of "soul travel" is similar to an "out-of-body" experience. This is said to be "taught only by the Living ECK Master" and made possible by more than 100 "spiritual exercises," such as visualization and chanting "HU" ("The most ancient, secret name for God"). During "soul travel" one can meet with dead ECK Masters and follow the Eck current back to the Sugmad.

Members, called *chelas*, pass through a series of initiations, the first of which "often comes in a dream." Controversy rocked the movement in the 1970s when its founder was accused of borrowing teachings from the Radhasoami Sant Mat tradition and plagiarizing the work of Julian Johnson (1873–1939), one of its disciples.

THEOSOPHY

KEY PERSON/FOUNDER, DATE, LOCATION

Theosophy is an esoteric philosophy and movement tracing its modern origin to Helena P. Blavatsky (1831–1891), also known as "Madame Blavatsky" or HPB. In 1875 she founded the Theosophical Society in New York with Henry Steel Olcott (1832–1907). Today there are two main groups, each known as the Theosophical Society, with one based in Adyar, India and one in Pasadena, California.

Helena P. Blavatsky

KEY BELIEFS

"Ancient wisdom" teachings hold that the world's religions (Greek, Egyptian, Christian, Gnostic, Buddhist, etc.) originally taught the same core truths, but were corrupted by the development of organized religion. The oldest scriptures (the Hindu *Vedas*) contain the kernel truths and the others carry parts of this core: pantheism, reincarnation, yoga, evolution of consciousness, psychic powers, etc.

WHO IS JESUS?

Jesus is considered the fifth incarnation in the Aryan race of the Christ, or supreme "World Teacher." Theosophy rejects Jesus' atonement and states that man brings about his own salvation through repeated incarnations; every human being is a potential "Christ."

OTHER FACTS, BELIEFS, OR PRACTICES

Invisible to us, the evolutionary progress of Earth has been directed for thousands of years by a seven-tiered hierarchy of Masters or superior beings. The Masters reveal themselves to a few select souls, giving guidance to those who are prepared for it. Blavatsky claimed to be in communication with several of these so-called Masters, as did most of her immediate successors.

Yoga and meditation are employed in spiritual development; psychic powers (including "easy access" to the mystic "Akashic Records"), astral travel, and other paranormal abilities may follow, depending on the individual. Astrology and some other occult practices are considered "true sciences."

An inner circle, known as the "Esoteric Section," engages in secret meditation practices to attune its members with the Masters. Theosophy became the fountainhead of the "ancient wisdom" doctrine within Western occultism, inspiring many other groups, including the Church Universal and Triumphant.

Key Writings

- Major works by Blavatsky, including
  - *Isis Unveiled* (1877)
  - *The Secret Doctrine* (1888)
  - *The Key to Theosophy* (1889)
- The periodical *Sunrise*

ANTHROPOSOPHY

KEY PERSON/FOUNDER, DATE, LOCATION

The Anthroposophical Society was founded in Germany in 1912 by Austrian psychic Rudolf Steiner (1861–1925) as a breakaway group from Theosophy. World headquarters located at the Goetheanum in Dornach, Switzerland.

Rudolf Steiner

KEY BELIEFS

Steiner claimed to receive information directly from the spiritual realm. Anthroposophy is based on his personal revelations, which describe an extremely complex evolutionary history for mankind. He began as a believer in Theosophy and embraced such Theosophical concepts as karma and reincarnation. Anthroposophy is relentlessly man-centered and pays little attention to traditional questions about "God" or our relationship to him.

Rejecting and Redefining Christianity

Though Steiner called his system "true Christianity," he also called it "Christian Occultism" and radically redefined Christian terms. Steiner saw the Bible not as revelation "from without," but as a picture of human potential. He describes two separate "Jesuses" who merged spiritually, after which a "Christ-essence" entered and remained for three years. At the crucifixion, Jesus' blood did not redeem us from sin, but flowed into the physical earth, where its mystical power energizes our cosmic evolution and frees us from the bonds of materialism. This enables the Christ-essence to "mass-incarnate" into the whole of humanity (which is the true "second coming").

OTHER FACTS, BELIEFS, OR PRACTICES

The central tenet of Anthroposophy is that humans have an ability to contact the spiritual realm directly, which can be awakened through exercises in concentration and meditation. The practice of Anthroposophy consists mostly of such exercises. Like all forms of occult meditation, this can open the door to intrusions from the unseen world, including spirit contact and associated phenomena, such as clairvoyance, divination, and mediumship.

Key Writings

All of Steiner's works are considered authoritative. This includes some 6,000 lectures, hundreds of essays, and 33 books, including

- *A Philosophy of Freedom* (1894)
- *Christianity as Mystical Fact* (1902)
- *An Outline of Occult Science* (1910)

First Goetheanum

Anthroposophy-related groups and activities include the Steiner-oriented Waldorf Schools movement, Weleda personal and healthcare products, and bio-dynamic farming (organic agriculture with magical/occult elements).

NEOPAGANISM AND WICCA

KEY PERSON/FOUNDER, DATE, LOCATION

No one founder or central organization. Roots in nineteenth-century Britain. Partly inspired by Margaret Murray (1863–1963) and organized by Gerald Gardner (1884–1964) in the 1930s to 1950s.

WHO IS GOD?

The supreme being is called the Goddess, sometimes the Goddess and God, or goddess and horned god ("Lord and Lady"). The Goddess can be a symbol, the impersonal force in everything, or a personal being. Wiccans can be pantheists, polytheists, or both.

WHO IS JESUS?

Jesus is either rejected altogether or sometimes considered a spiritual teacher who taught love and compassion.

WHO IS THE HOLY SPIRIT?

The Holy Spirit is not part of this belief. However, some Wiccans may refer to "Spirit" as a kind of divine energy.

HOW TO BE SAVED

Wiccans do not believe that humanity is sinful or needs saving. It is important for Wiccans to honor and work for the preservation of nature (which they equate with the Goddess).

WHAT HAPPENS AFTER DEATH?

The body replenishes the earth, which is the Goddess's wish. Some Wiccans are agnostic about life after death, others believe in reincarnation. Some believe in a wonderful place called Summerland.

OTHER FACTS, BELIEFS, OR PRACTICES

Wiccans practice divination and spell-casting, with most rituals performed in a circle. Many Wiccans are part of a coven (local assembly), though many others are "solitary." Covens meet for ritual and seasonal holidays, including the eight major holidays (such as Vernal Equinox, Summer Solstice, and Beltane). Wicca is an occultic "nature religion," not Satanism.

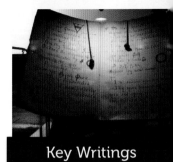

Key Writings

- No holy books; many groups use *The Book of Shadows*, first compiled by Gardner and later expanded.

- Other popular works:
  - » *The Spiral Dance* by Starhawk (1979)
  - » *A Witches' Bible* by Janet and Stewart Farrar (1981)

Autumn equinox (Mabon) celebration at Stonehenge

FREEMASONRY

KEY PERSON/FOUNDER, DATE, LOCATION

No one founder or central organization. Freemasonry is a secret society which claims descent from the stonemasons of medieval Europe or Solomon's Temple, but which actually started in London in 1717 as a "lodge" with initiations, symbols, and degrees. Masons pass the Blue Lodge first and may continue into Scottish Rite or York Rite. In the United States, the Grand Lodge of each state is the highest authority.

KEY WRITINGS

- Ceremonies often employ a Bible, but may use other "holy books" instead
- Popular writings:

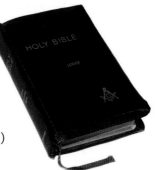

  - » *The Builders* by Joseph Fort Newton (1914)
  - » *Introduction to Freemasonry* by Carl Claudy (1931)
  - » *Coil's Masonic Encyclopedia* (1961)
  - » *Mackey's Revised Masonic Encyclopedia* (1966)
- The Grand Lodge of each state publishes a "monitor" (description and commentary) of its rituals

KEY BELIEFS

Masonry claims to transmit secret teachings from ancient times. The "Masonic Edition" of the Bible says, "Masonry is descended from the ancient mysteries." Masonry requires belief in a Supreme Being and treats all religions as though they believe in the same God, whom Masons call by such titles as "Great Architect of the Universe" and "Jah-Bul-On" (supposedly his "secret name").

Loyalty binds Masons to one another, and Masons promise by oath of gory death never to reveal their secret rituals to outsiders (curses that are symbolic today). Masonic vows include protection to fellow Masons, even in cases of crime.

OCCULTIC INFLUENCES

Evangelical researchers John Ankerberg and John Weldon state that Masonry serves as an introduction to the occult because, among other reasons, "in symbolism and philosophy it is similar to many occult practices," and because it is "a system of mysticism which accepts the development of altered states of consciousness."

Who Is Jesus?

When the Bible is quoted, references to Jesus are omitted; public prayers must not use Jesus' name. In several rituals Jesus is made equal to Zoroaster, Buddha, or Muhammad. Salvation to the "Grand Lodge above" is achieved by living an upright life, without explicit faith in Christ.

Masonic recommended readings for advanced degrees include works by pagan/occult authors.

ROSICRUCIANISM (AMORC)

KEY PERSON/FOUNDER, DATE, LOCATION

Said to be founded by Christian Rosenkreuz ("rosy cross"), a legendary occultist probably invented in 1614 by Johann Valentin Andreae (1586–1654). Europe spawned many Rosicrucian lodges. The largest group today is the Ancient Mystical Order Rosae Crucis (AMORC)—or simply Rosicrucian Order—founded in 1915 by H. Spencer Lewis (1883–1939). Headquartered in San Jose, California, AMORC has claimed hundreds of thousands of members in over 100 countries.

Johann Valentin Andreae

KEY WRITINGS

- *Mastery of Life* (an introductory booklet)
- Popular books by Lewis include
  - » *The Mystical Life of Jesus* (1929)
  - » *Mansions of the Soul* (1930)
  - » *The Secret Doctrines of Jesus* (1937)
- *Rosicrucian Digest* (published quarterly)
- *Rosicrucian Forum* (for members only)
- Inner teachings are disclosed to initiates through secret "monographs" sent by mail, as well as by lectures, directed studies, and members-only gatherings

KEY BELIEFS

To AMORC, the Bible is neither unique nor reliable. AMORC literature is openly hostile to Christianity and specifically rejects Christian teachings on God, Christ, salvation, and a host of other key doctrines. Supposedly anyone can use the group's principles, regardless of church or religion. The advertised goal of life is "mastery of the self." The keys to one's spiritual transformation are buried in many places: Egyptian religions, Hinduism, kabbalah, gnosticism, and Gnostic Christianity.

Students use mental techniques to actualize their focused thoughts of health, prosperity, peace, and happiness. Belief in karma, reincarnation, and a "Great White Brotherhood" of highly evolved spiritual masters.

Alchemical and planetary symbolism in Rosicrucian diagram

Other Facts, Beliefs, or Practices

AMORC offers a blend of necromancy, mysticism, and Egyptian religion with "development of such psychic powers as telepathy, telekinesis, radiesthesia, clairvoyance, clairaudience, and psychic projection." Occult rituals employ mirrors, incense, candles, herbs, and similar paraphernalia. The AMORC-related Traditional Martinist Order studies mystical symbols and the Kabbalah.

THE CHURCH OF SATAN/SATANISM

KEY PERSON/FOUNDER, DATE, LOCATION

First Church of Satan was founded by Anton Szandor LaVey (1930–1997) in San Francisco, California, in 1966. Many Satanic groups have modeled themselves on the Church of Satan.

Key Writings

- *The Satanic Bible* (1969)
- *The Satanic Witch* (1971)
- Other works by LaVey

KEY BELIEFS

Satanism thoroughly and forcefully rejects biblical Christian doctrine and ethics and is man-centered in the extreme. God is viewed as an impersonal balancing force of nature; LaVey writes that those who believe in a literal God invented him as an externalized form of their own ego. Jesus is regarded as either mythical or a failure.

There are "Nine Satanic Statements," or principles, some of which are: Man should indulge, not abstain; be kind only to the deserving; and take vengeance instead of turning the other cheek ("Do unto others as they do unto you"). Satanists look down on those who want to do good, calling them "white-lighters."

OTHER FACTS, BELIEFS, OR PRACTICES

Satanic magic is based primarily on desire, manipulation, imagery, and force of will done in ritual. For the Satanist, there is no such thing as "black or white magick"; there is only magic. LaVey wrote that "Satanic Ritual is a blend of Gnostic, Cabbalistic, Hermetic, and Masonic elements" employing "vibratory words of power."

Some Satanists perform a blasphemous ceremony known as the "black mass." The most important holidays are the Satanist's own birthday, April 30th (climax of spring equinox), and October 31st.

Satan's Place in Satanism

While some Satanists believe that Satan is a real, personal being, those who follow LaVey's teachings usually do not. Instead, Satan symbolizes man as his own god and opposition to all religions. Man is just another animal and should be free of moral codes. Belief in sin is designed to make men feel guilty so that they can be controlled by hypocritical religious systems. Though man should learn from his mistakes, there is no need for salvation. There is no life beyond death; life is to be lived now, vitally and pleasurably.

VOODOO

KEY PERSON/FOUNDER, DATE, LOCATION

No one founder or central organization. Voodoo—also spelled *vodun* **and** *vodou* (from the Fon *vodu*, "spirit" or "deity")—was brought by West African slaves to colonial Haiti, where it is now the dominant religion. It first entered the United States after the Haitian Revolution of 1791–1804.

KEY WRITINGS

None. Voodoo's beliefs and practices are based primarily on oral traditions and vary from place to place.

KEY BELIEFS

Haitian voodoo is an animistic religion and combines many elements of African cults, Roman Catholic imagery and ritual, and even European folklore. There are two main types of voodoo: *Rada* (seen by practitioners as benign) and *Petro* (seen as dominated by black magic). Voodoo acknowledges a remote creator god, called *Bondye*.

After death, one part of man's spirit goes to Bondye, and another goes to

Gine (a kind of African spiritual homeland); there is also a belief in reincarnation.

OTHER FACTS, BELIEFS, OR PRACTICES

Spirits, summoned ritually by drums, are said to "mount" (possess) worshipers like horses, speaking and acting through them. Various kinds of divination and sorcery are used for protection, healing, direction, luck, and inflicting harm on enemies. Ritual offerings—including food, drink, and animal sacrifices—are made to appease the spirits. Cemeteries are important to some rituals. "New Orleans Voodoo" is a distinct expression practiced mainly in Louisiana and related to local "Hoodoo" folk magic.

Spirits

Humans must deal with three main types of spirits: *lemistè* (also known as *loa* or *lwa*), *lemó* (the dead), and *lemarasa* (the sacred twins). There are thousands of the capricious *lwa*, among the most important of which are *Ezili* (associated with Our Lady of Mt. Carmel, love, and beauty) and *Dambala* (associated with St. Patrick and snakes).

SANTERÍA

KEY PERSON/FOUNDER, DATE, LOCATION

No one founder. Santería (from the Spanish, "way of the saints")—also called *lucumí* and *Regla de Ocha*—comes primarily from the religion of the Yoruba people of southwestern Nigeria, who were brought to Cuba in the sixteenth–nineteenth centuries as slaves. Santería was mainly brought to the United States by Cubans fleeing Fidel Castro's regime.

KEY WRITINGS

None. Santería's beliefs and practices are based primarily on oral traditions and vary from place to place. Some of the most authoritative written descriptions are Spanish-language works by Cuban author Lydia Cabrera, especially *El Monte* (1954).

KEY BELIEFS

Santería is an animistic religion but has many Roman Catholic followers. Santería acknowledges a remote creator god, called *Olofi* or *Olodumare*.

Jesus is considered to have been "a great sorcerer." *Ashé* is considered a neutral cosmic energy. Santería teaches reincarnation.

OTHER FACTS, BELIEFS, OR PRACTICES

Santería has been described as "jungle magic adapted to city living." Diviners use cowrie shells, coconuts, and other sacred objects to identify and solve personal problems. Spirit possession occurs frequently in group rituals, which can also include animal blood sacrifices (mostly chickens and goats) and the use of various herbs and plants. Sacred stones (*otanes*) and various talismans thought to possess great spiritual power are also used.

Spirits

Followers must placate a variety of capricious spirits, including dozens of lesser deities (*orishas* or *orichás*) and spirits of the dead (including ancestors, slaves, Indians, and gypsies). Orishas are associated with forces of nature and with Roman Catholic saints (*santos*). The main orishas are known as the *Siete Potencias Africanas* (seven African powers), each having its own elaborate mythology.

Why Should Christians Study Other Religions?

The New Testament offers us two kinds of examples.

First, in Acts 17 the apostle Paul engaged with the non-Christian religions of his day. Paul understood their beliefs well enough to quote their spiritual authorities (see verses 24–28), and his knowledge built bridges to help their followers understand the gospel.

Second, in their epistles Paul, Peter, John, and Jude engaged with the counterfeit gospels of their day. In order to warn and instruct Christians about the teachings of false apostles and

prophets, these New Testament writers had to be familiar with their claims.

In today's world, Jesus' followers are faced with more religious groups than ever before. As we seek to understand these groups, the motives and methods of the apostles and the other authors of Scripture are our best model for ministry.

What Some Groups Teach about Jesus and the Bible's Response

WHAT OTHERS TEACH	WHAT THE BIBLE SAYS
Jesus was not God.	John 1:1–18; 8:56–58; Colossians 1:15–20; 1 Timothy 3:16
Jesus was created by God.	Isaiah 7:14; Matthew 1:18; John 10:30–38; 17:5
There are three separate gods: Father, Son, and Holy Spirit, not one God in three persons.	Deuteronomy 6:4; Isaiah 43:10; 44:6–8; Matthew 28:18–19; John 10:30–38; Hebrews 1:1–14
Jesus is not necessary because there is no sin.	John 3:14–17; Romans 3:23–30; 6:23; 1 John 1:8–10
Jesus was not raised bodily from the dead.	Luke 24:36–53; Acts 1:11; 1 Corinthians 15:1–23
Jesus was a great prophet, but not God.	Matthew 1:18; John 5:17–18, 23; 10:30–38; Colossians 2:9–10
There are many ways to God, not just one.	John 3:14–17; 14:6–7; 1 Timothy 2:5–6
Jesus is not necessary because people must pay for their own sins.	John 17:2–3; Romans 6:23; 10:3–10; Ephesians 2:8–9
Jesus died for sins, but people can't be saved unless they obey all the teachings of the church.	John 14:6–7; Romans 10:3–10; Ephesians 2:8–9
Jesus is God, but less than God the Father.	John 5:17–23; 14:6–7; Colossians 2:9–10
Jesus was just a man.	Isaiah 7:14; Matthew 1:18; John 2:18–22; 10:30–38
Jesus is not the only son of God.	John 3:14–17; Hebrews 1:1–14
Jesus will never come again.	Acts 1:11; 1 Thessalonians 4:13–18

MADE EASY

by Rose Publishing

The *Made Easy* series helps you quickly find biblical answers to important questions. These pocket-sized books are packed with clear explanations and key facts you need to know.

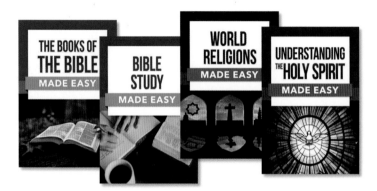

THE BOOKS OF THE BIBLE MADE EASY
Quick summaries of all 66 books of the Bible
ISBN 9781628623420

BIBLE STUDY MADE EASY
A step-by-step guide to studying God's Word
ISBN 9781628623437

WORLD RELIGIONS MADE EASY
30 religions and how they compare to Christianity
ISBN 9781628623451

UNDERSTANDING THE HOLY SPIRIT MADE EASY
Who the Holy Spirit is and what he does
ISBN 9781628623444

HENDRICKSON PUBLISHERS   ROSE PUBLISHING

www.hendricksonrose.com